ETERNALLY CRYPTIC WORKS
Second Edition

Pablo Weston

Cover by Nhi Nguyen

TABLE OF CONTENTS

Eternally Cryptic Works

THE DEGENERATES' HANDBOOK

THE PALINDROMES OF PARLIAMENT

To demonstrate my freedom of speech,
First, I must un-mute my voice.
Then, to the ballot-goers, I shall teach
Of the illusion they call choice.
Privileged and privately pampered,
Then into a party they're procured,
Are both sets of inbred wankers
Sending pamphlets through your doors.

Though there's some minute opposition,
See how seamlessly they switch team,
For if they fulfil their dystopian vision
Then both their beds they would cream;
A world of lifetimes spent in servitude
To fund their wars through your tax,
So with a change, yourselves, do not delude
For it's the same face, different mask.

I won't participate in such apathy
For it's archaic, and I believe,
Those who try to halt its catastrophe,
Though good-intentioned, are naive.
They can't see its flaws or limitations, nor
It's a pantomime, they actors,
And no substantial change can be made for
They're exactly the same; backwards.

IN THE TWINKLING OF AN EYE

In the twinkling of an eye,
Whilst content and snug in bed,
Look up to a sequined supernal shine
Bedazzling high overhead.
In the twinkling of an eye,
Whilst trapped by a world terrene,
Allow the bright empyreal light
To carry you to a dream.

In the squinting of an eye,
Seeing way over yonder,
See not the darkness eclipse the light
But fill your sights with wonder.
In the squinting of an eye,
Notice how the sparkle's brief,
And see that nothing's impossible
If you possess self-belief.

In the blinking of an eye,
The world could forget your name,
For if you wish to clone your ancestors,
What of you will remain?
In the blinking of an eye,
You could wake up to be dead,
If you live your dreams just in your mind
Whilst cemented to your bed.

In the twinkling of an eye,
You could reach enlightenment,
By learning to walk the chosen path,
Which is your entitlement.
In the twinkling of an eye,
There's everything that can be,
And your life is but some stepping stones
You must walk to help you see.

THE WEIGHT OF THE WORLD

See how the beauteous petals unfold,
Emerging 'neath pervading hallowed light, -
And see how their splendrous hue shimmers gold
Like a treasure to each admirer's sight.
Stay watchful of how they pullulate Earth
With ambrosial scents whilst you're woebegone,
And fulfil potential, proving their worth -
Rather than greet Time's vapid rubicon.
Know that their beauty you must replicate,
Whatever form you take, it must fluoresce,
And sacrifice your life to add your weight,
Giving a purpose to the purposeless, -
As suns eclipse and flowers decompose
Once Ambition's solipsist lids shut close.

MEDUSA'S MIRROR

Your ophidian locks, with minds abject,
And grisly teratoid tongues sibilate
Their whisperings of doubt and loathsome hate
Until your waxen mind they misdirect,
So that your aspirations you neglect,
And think your pallid cheeks are roseate,
As they further gird and manipulate
So that your bloodshot orbs don't introspect
To see the ugly truth and be aghast
At not appearing how they said you would,
For they know your mortal flagitious past,
With a glance would be sacrificed for good;
That their corrosive stone will not outlast
The winged-children spawned from your gorgon blood.

THE MOLTEN IN THE MELTING POT

The molten in the melting pot
(Refusing to assimilate),
Untouchable and scorching hot,
Dripping on the memories forged is...
The molten in the melting pot.

To conquer, they must first divide
(If they have not divided themselves).
For should they become unified,
A sword born of their core will be cast
To conquer that which does divide.

POPPY FIELDS

All your heroes are made from human shields,
Pridefully loyal to the oath they've sworn
(To further sow Her precious poppy fields).

Never to know how murder looks or feels,
You praise their deeds, blissfully unaware
All your heroes are made from human shields.

Reaping comfortably with un-muddied hands,
The bloodthirsty leaders bloodstain the pawn
(To further sow Her precious poppy fields).

The idolizing youth, brainwashed and brawn,
March skywards from battle, and nobly know,
All your heroes are made from human shields.

As mothers mourn whilst the mortal still squeals,
In your bellicose eyes, revenge does spawn
(To further sow Her precious poppy fields).

Like a bullet-wounded heart never heals -
The tragic truth, on you, will never dawn:
All your heroes are made from human shields
(To further sow Her precious poppy fields).

TO LEARN

Open valves to the reservoir of Thought
And let its scintillating current bless.
Then once illumination has been brought,
See that vagrancy is virtuousness.
Be willing to forget all you've been taught.
Forever cultivate, and thus progress.
Allow your ego to dissolve, and see
Knowledge has no place for Authority.

Wander through the garden of Intellect,
Where vines of Truth adorn and embower
You, so whomever sides or does object,
Your integrity, you don't deflower.
Then, only once perfection you accept,
The fruits of Humbleness can you devour, -
And should true genius evoke your name,
Revere the source from whence it came.

GREEN PLANET

Peek at my garden's verdure
And be lifted to the realm of godly sights,
Only then to be further
Charioted to Heaven's bountiful heights,
Which you may choose whether you want to see, -
With prideful unrelinquished sovereignty.

You'll die as you were born: free!
So you're free to shun my gift of sight, and fan
Rising flames of Liberty;
Free to think you can control your fellow man
And free to claim my lands you possess -
But you can't delude sovereign Consciousness.

ILLUSIONS

A social construct is nothing more than deception en masse,
Which has you ruled and regimented into your respective class.
They pump out propaganda aimed to dampen your defiance,
As their existence is reliant solely on your compliance.

Orthodoxy catalyses an authoritarian
To pose as an activist to further your delirium,
Punching pacifists for that old pipsqueak on the podium:
"Ignoring what I say is inciting pandemonium!"

Powerless, you're humbled by this hobgoblin's harangue,
As you know sugarcoated ants shouldn't lust for meringue.
Ah, laws don't prevent murders - but it is your free will
That determines who, and when, and why, and what we kill.

Mawkishness is mimicked by the man you voted for
But what's not a hokey gimmick, and which you mutually adore,
Is the polarisation, limitations, the lifelong bait;
Money: the God that never has and never will create.

A social construct is nothing more than deception en masse,
Which has you ruled and regimented into your respective class.
They pump out propaganda aimed to dampen your defiance,
As their existence is reliant solely on your compliance.

A BRAIN FOR THE BETTERMENT OF BILLIONS

For every problem there's a solution,
Though their seeking's problematic when you're blind, -
And so too is the dream of a global revolution
If you don't hold love for humankind.
Perhaps your avidity is as lilliputian
As those dreamers who, this world, designed,
Perhaps you're consumed by pessimism
At the mere mentioning of altruism,
Or you don't believe through pragmatism,
A change, we could mastermind.
Maybe you've mistook misery for maturity,
And have always done what you're told you're aught
Unquestionably, filled with fear and insecurity, -
Thinking Peace is something for which must be fought.
My dear, perhaps you've simply never thought.

Of course, by past failings we must be taught
If we're to dismantle this juggernaut,
And of course it would be foolish for me to claim
I can provide every answer for our subsistence,
Considering the brevity of our existence,
And the puny size of my sole human brain, -
But, in a certain way, I'm the messiah;
My mission is to make you think.
I'm not content on preaching to the choir,
I'm intent, with this page and ink
To belief, in you, inspire,
And some of your fears allay, -
Fears, parroting what others say:

A BRAIN FOR THE BETTERMENT OF BILLIONS

Indeed, these hopes are ideological
But, as a complaint, that's quite illogical,
For every system, I'm sure you'll find,
Arose as figments from someone's mind.
Your other concerns are more legit,
Like not wanting criminals to recommit
Crimes like glorifying greed
When half the world's in desperate need
By ravishing lavish wine and meat
Whilst rationing what you can eat,
When in this moment you're well-fed,
Have dry clothes and a comfy bed,
And though you know there's whole lands populated
Where their faces are emaciated, -
At least you don't have to see any of the dead.

But this is not a reason for, to Change, cower -
It's just proof a hierarchical structure of power
Inevitably leads to disparity and thus mistrust,
For every past crime they did,
A revolutionary usurped the same crooked pyramid
So to (and from) a powerless world we must adjust;
Greed we can no longer lust
If us and more are to be well-fed, -
A leaderless world is how we must be led.
Now wipe those tears from your eyes!
Wipe those fears from your eyes!
Just because the future holds uncertainty,
Is not a reason to not fervently
Seek the improvements we need urgently
If we're not to devolve.
As we have the power to determinedly
Every problem solve.

A BRAIN FOR THE BETTERMENT OF BILLIONS

Yet, you still have fear in your heart
Which your ego fears will be torn apart
As, when they whimperingly die,
There'll be no mournful tears for you to cry.
Oh, have no fear! Have no fear!
I am your messiah, the end is near,
And all the fright in your head fluttering
Is the echoes of their threats stuttering,
Like what the sheep-dog may do if you flee the herd,
Well I've been sent to tell you - don't be scared;
You have nothing to fear about dissent,
What's terrifying is if you try to cement
This ghastly tyranny who are hellbent
On perpetuating this feared state,
Where your entire life they dictate.
Yes, me they will try to defame,
As my message they can not.
But a life of riches and fame
Is not integral to my plot;
Through every past regret they can try to shame
Me as if I am supposed to be more than a man,
They can torture and they can maim,
And my existence they can swat -
But there's no torture worse than not
Existing as exactly who I am -
And if my messianic origins
Equate to mercilessly punished sins;
If we were truly doomed to this fate since our birth,
Then at least we'll know Heaven's not a place on Earth.

A BRAIN FOR THE BETTERMENT OF BILLIONS

It is your fear which gives them power,
It is the vital ingredient the domineering devour;
Your disobedience you need not hide,
Tell them the truth loud with pride,
And once we're the majority in this game,
To us all, they can't do the same.
Your fear is what gives them hope,
And is the root of every insane excuse,
All pretending the simple is quite abstruse,
And behaving like a misanthrope.
Yes, the rapist, psycho, and terrorist,
As they do now, may still exist
But why would this be a reason to resist
Change, and instead persist
With the world in which they were devised
For any reason other than Fear has you hypnotised?
It's a complex world - but my message is quite plain:
You have the freedom to use your brain.
So think! Think what world you want to build!
One where you can make the choice to be fulfilled
Or one where fear is instilled,
Where for telling the truth, you think you'll be killed;
The choice between
A utopia or dystopia, heaven or hell...
But I will let you on all you've seen,
Rather than simply tell,
Decide if you'd like to dream this dream
As well, or deeper into brimstone sink,
Enflamed where demons dwell.
No, I will let you decide
Down which path yourself will guide,
Leaving Humanity's footprints with every stride,
To reap the consequences of your ambition,
Just remember I've just one mission, -
My mission is to make you think.

A BRAIN FOR THE BETTERMENT OF BILLIONS

Think! Think!
Feel your heart sink
As you see your leaders lick their lips
At the thought of an apocalypse.
Think back to the famished unfortunate,
Those, supposedly your coordinate,
Spot how your wealth is disproportionate,
And see how skeletal are their hips...
As others die from eating too much chips.
Would you not prefer
To save a life and your feast share,
And their dying wishes heed,
Rather than, again, glorifying greed?
Together, every prince and prole
Could make it out combined goal
To, without too much rigmarole
Have every soul in desperate need
Be able to themselves and others feed -
But if this system is to be maintained,
Not everyone can be sustained.
For there's no possibility
It could function without incivility,
For its very shape is conoid
So in the unlikelihood all were employed
Rising prices we could not avoid,
So the starving and nobility
Shall forever be an inevitability.
Ah, think! Think of how we can progress,
Combining our minds and using our wisdom
To conjure up a working system.
No, don't allow it to continue to depress.

A BRAIN FOR THE BETTERMENT OF BILLIONS

Think! Think!
Feel your heart sink
As you see the peckish flies
Swarm atop red and yellow eyes,
With helpless onlookers unable to aid,
Hearing coughing and shivering, afraid
That from this Earthly kingdom they'll too fade -
And once yet another victim dies,
Some will wag their fingers at the skies,
But rather than see people endure
Illnesses, for which, we have the cure
Would it not be wiser to devote
Our time to sharing each antidote
And realise the power's in our hands
To heal the feeble in these sickly lands, -
Or is helping not in our plans
More than it is our health and wealth to gloat?
Ah, perhaps you think they'll be cured by a vote!
Now, I don't want to be called a pessimist -
But such false hopes must be dismissed.
For Truth is what this doctor orders
If haleness is to reach all quarters.
As whomever mounts the same foundations,
Would too fall victim to its limitations,
- As have millennia of generations,
And be forced to be resource-hoarders,
With their imaginary money and imaginary borders.

A BRAIN FOR THE BETTERMENT OF BILLIONS

Now, look closer to your home,
And think of all you could bemoan:
Think as poisons are sold to drink
As before screens their eyes seldom blink,
And pupils shrivel as brains shrink,
And some with Fame are rewarded
To glamorise sins most sordid.
Think! Think!
Think if Wisdom were to be revered
And all oafishness disappeared
How this world with joys could glare,
Begemming the current darkness and despair,
And if we stopped mimicking all we see,
Disbanding the fruitless world of celebrity -
Perhaps music, art, and poetry
Would be hoisted from their sepulchre,
As for money and Fame, - Art has no care.
Take a look at the rampant suicide
Surrounding you from every side,
And tell me with a straight face
That's because the world's such a pleasant place,
Where people are free to do as they please
And aren't in servitude and on their knees,
Where their parents' wishes, they're wished to appease,
And this simple truth, they address:
Freedom is the only path to Happiness.

A BRAIN FOR THE BETTERMENT OF BILLIONS

Think! Think!
Feel your heart sink
As you see your leaders lick their lips
At the thought of an apocalypse.
At how murderously without mercy,
The Ganges, Hudson, Thames, and Mersey
Could all with blood become dirty,
Where bones could float along like the River Styx
If we choose these problems not to fix!
See how, with your precious tax,
They stockpile sarin, ebola, and anthrax,
How without a moments haste
They pollute Nature with nuclear waste.
See how with no remorse
They straddle the galloping Red Horse -
How innumerable lives have been lost on their course;
See how no one's disgraced
To say war should never be erased.
They're the antithesis
Of peacefulness,
And any thought that they'll be changed
I'm afraid is borderline deranged;
The crimes for which you consent,
And which they carry out with merriment,
Not a soul can prevent
When winnings they can yield
Every time weapons we wield
Or someone's skin is peeled
Faraway on a foreign field.

A BRAIN FOR THE BETTERMENT OF BILLIONS

Plus, even if they wished to change
(Which they don't),
They'd have to succeed at diplomacy
(Which they won't);
Convincing over a hundred different teams.
Each with a different ideology,
To meet out their pacifistic dreams -
Even when it means
They'll earn less gold,
And after four years hope all uphold
When the dices are rerolled,
With paranoia over who will fold.
Only then, could we forever more
Live in this eternal war, -
Whilst it's hawkishly cold.
But think! Think of how we can progress,
Combining our minds and using our wisdom
To conjure up a working system.
No, don't allow it to continue to depress.
Think of all the unmentionable things,
In which your mind springs;
The uncountable amount I've failed to say
Which we all witness every day, -
And feel the rising ripples in your voice
Say of how it's just a choice,
How in this fact we can rejoice,
And though one person won't lead the way,
Together, -
Together the pendulum our thoughts will sway!

A BRAIN FOR THE BETTERMENT OF BILLIONS

War, hunger, slavery, if we obey
The gargoyles of the government,
Then the sobering reality, - to our dismay,
Is that none will see their abolishment.
'So if on these phoney leaders we can't rely'
I hear your newborn pondering aloud
'Who will be the vox populi
To bring concord to the crowd?'
Well, the answer is you, and me, and everyone
Who is blessed with the gift to think;
Whomever wherever illumination has shone
And revealed the darkness has a chink.
So, as just one of those billions, some solutions I'll give -
And ideas how to implement each alternative:
In thraldom we shall always live
For as long as there's a price on every crumb.
Yet, the census of mouths and food to yield,
Is quite a simple mathematical sum.
The complexity comes from deciding how
We will plant and distribute
With equal efficiency (and more equally than now)
And have in place a reliable substitute.
I suggest self-sufficiency such a trouble could mend
And, in fact, for many of our problems could be a panacea,
For it seems unwise on one source to solely depend, -
With the naivete that Nature in our plans shan't interfere.

A BRAIN FOR THE BETTERMENT OF BILLIONS

A leaderless world to every change is key
For, quite ironically, anarchy
Is the truest form of democracy, -
And with the internet's interconnectivity
Each problem can be tossed to a billion brains
Rather than just an elite few,
And if altruism truly runs through their veins,
They'd be participating too, -
Without the limitations they had before,
And their integrity being plundered,
And without the inventions of nations - gun crime's not called war
And neither is it funded.
Without money, crime's reduced and your ambitions are roused
Whilst, due to every desolate corporation,
More people could be housed
And none would be lacking in privation.
Without a leader, we can have no corruption.
And the apathetic shall cause their own destruction
In a system where all can participate
To decide upon our species' fate.
My idea is eternal malleability,
And I believe it's a possibility
And that towards perfection we can move
If on imperfections we always improve,
If every institution is keelhauled
And we place pleasantries where we were once appalled;
In a world where the law is Love.

A BRAIN FOR THE BETTERMENT OF BILLIONS

Think, and see no war's needed for us to move
From anguish into Eden;
We don't need any serpent to approve
Of us happily choosing Freedom.
Love! Love! This is the golden rule;
That if every decision's not for all's betterment
It can only cause detriment, -
And could only come from a fool.
When more and more as people we are loving,
Less and less is the need to be governed.
So love, and with Love's gift of Wisdom,
Help to conjure up a working system
That spins revolutions in your thinking head.
Just don't question from whose words it's being led.

CELTIC REVISIONARIES

WELL WORTH THE WAIT

The sun shines hot, as the weed inside my sock
Steadily starts to chafe -
But our bags are packed,
As we bobble on the tracks -
We know it will be well worth the wait.

I've fantasized innumerable times
To wake up to see your nitid face gleaming.
So you can count the sheep
If it helps you get to sleep
But I'll still pinch you when you're dreaming.

Where dragons once roared
And in stones, men stuck swords,
We will be cast to estivate.
Flabbergasted by the views
And the cacophonies of your snooze,
I know it will be well worth the wait.

We can rhapsodize about the past lives
Of martyrs, monks, and the clergy,
And what gifts they'd bestow
To show knowledge that they know
And, if in this present, their presents seem worthy.

Oh, how when we were paired,
We were unprepared to serve the masters of our fate
But now, with this Machynlleth switch,
Our destinies will not drift,
And we know it will be worth the wait.

WELL WORTH THE WAIT

Like a Grandfather's clock,
Or a Granddaughter's watch,
You just can't stop the times from moving,
So I smile and count the stops
And laugh as pennies drop
For I know the beginning of the end is looming.

I lick my lips as my eagerness persists,
Though I know history won't record this date,
So in my mind, where there's no time,
I will assemble for you a shrine -
As your existence was well worth the wait.

Don't be scared of explosions in Space
For it's just a relay race,
So take it in your stride like a starlet,
Know that, again, we'll witness the sunshine
As we reach the finish line -
And we'll be greeted by the beauty of Harlech.

THE ALARM BELLS OF THE COUNTRYSIDE

Sound the alarm bells of the countryside,
And may there sprightly emerge in a gust,
A lullaby for all those far and wide.

As ancient sirens serenade with pride,
With their desire immortal as dust,
Sound the alarm bells of the countryside.

Wantonly sung: "A tongue will further glide,
Mouth-watering, eager to mount her bust";
A lullaby for all those far and wide.

As, rosy-cheeked, she wants a place to hide
To feel Time make her reputation rust.
Sound the alarm bells of the countryside,

For some pleasures refuse to subside.
Humming loud, with proud palpitating Lust,
A lullaby for all those far and wide.

VERTIGO

I'm the paragon of calm till I reach a cliff,
Then my mind begins to wonder 'what if?'
And all my ponderings I just can't control,
I feel like a pirate has hijacked my soul.

I think there's a reason as to why I exist,
Then my mind begins to wonder 'what if?'
I close my eyes and pray I'll soon find a cure
To these maddening ailments, I must endure.

I'm incapable of nothing; I know that I can -
But what if I'm not even the person I think I am?
For I feel in my heart I don't want to die
But as my feet retreat backwards, my mind wants to fly.

MY CITRONELLA

Oh, my citronella, can one shepherd your flame?
Its mesmeric flicker astounds me!
An upsurge of flushness, I'm unable to tame
As I gaze at you most profoundly.
Your citrus-scented balm, also alluring,
Fumigates my woes.
Your cherubic charms, I won't cease adoring
(Or at least while I'm living I suppose).
Naked at the peril of a marauding parasite,
I nuzzle your warmth for protection.
Me too, blinded by your beaconed light,
Ascended highest for your affection.
Now my eyes flicker against your flame,
Amongst your fragrance I breathe my last breath,
And now I know that just to be with you, my love,
Is more heavenly than death.

I WANT TO LIVE

I confess that I too was born an animal, -
An animal shielded from its instincts -
But, if I was starved, I'd become a cannibal
Regardless of what moral observers would think!
An animal who would crush every single bug,
And even wrestle with a whale,
Yet an animal you wouldn't assume to be a thug
For it wears intellect as its veil.

Since I was a baby, my fears ran rife -
It's not a myth that I would run from the dead
Long before I knew how to crawl...
But to continue this pursuit of life,
Like a matryoshka doll, my fears I had to shed,
And see Death lay beneath them all.

SITTING ON A MOUNTAINTOP

To colossal rivers, I'm just a speck,
Who to glimpse their might, overawes my lips, -
And I must arch my back and cramp my neck
If I'm to see the flashing towers' tips,
Which twinkle far beneath this godly throne,
Above smoky clouds, under star-filled skies -
Which astound me as I watch all alone,
So much, that I'm forced to soliloquise:
"How can ephemeral souls earnestly
Believe in our importance when we're small,
And even this mountain will certainly
Meet Fate and be eclipsed by you all?"
Then I look down, and it occurs to me -
You're only as great as your eyes can see.

THE RAINIEST NIGHT EVER

Gilgamesh, you boast of puddles!
Noah, of your canoe!
That night her shouting caused the seas to rise
Above the peaks of Kathmandu.
All because I tried to share some fudge,
Equally, two by two.

Unfortunately, for me, no-one did soothsay,
Nor tell me what to do.
My promethean eyes scanned for Parnassus
As the deluge did ensue.
Though salvation was not a stone's throw away
(Unlike those other two).

Bickers and lies incessantly poured
As I thought 'These myths can't be true!'
Then, from above, Valhalla crumbled
And our world was born anew.
In disbelief, we'd survived the Ragnarök -
Now soggy lay we two.

THE CULT OF PORTMEIRION

As I observed with watchful eyes,
A crookback rose, to my surprise,
Then returned to the hole in which he lurked,
Once he'd said "Good day!" with a smirk.
In the sunlit oasis, just beyond his reach,
Lay a splendrous fountain, most antique.
Also resplendent in the rays,
Were the flowers of prismatic shades,
With optic verve, they did erupt
Till their beauty a father did obstruct,
To take a freaky family photo, -
Souring the taste of my cocoa.
Through the archway, onto the coiled streets,
Curiosity did increase;
Italianate houses, most pristine,
Without an owner to be seen -
I pondered, 'What sane mind would construct
A treasure only to gather dust?
And who would reside in such a town
That closes its gates when the sun goes down?'
Suddenly, there stood a cicerone.
His smile, too, freaky – but also phoney.
With maniacal eyes, he scorned
The very role which he performed -
But what further unhinged my brain
Was when he expected his bus, I entrain.
Clambering over garbage to reach my seat,
As with drowsiness, I did compete.
Then, he looked at my cocoa, and started to drive -
His wild-eyes asking 'Is he still alive?'

THE CULT OF PORTMEIRION

When I woke up, above me stood
A hooded coterie in Devil's Wood.
"Where are the rhododendrons?" My voice slurred.
"Beyond this cloistral setting, where you can't be heard!"
My limbs were tied as the lauding commenced.
In shock, I heard them tirade against
The excessive amount of people with limbs,
Whilst removing their clothes to reveal their fins, -
Explaining all the mermaid iconography
(Though their droopy-nipples still seemed odd to me).
That was, until they revealed to me,
The gardeners I had longed to see:
Their fingers were dirty, crooked and cut,
They'd been enslaved and whipped like a mutt,
And had nipple clamps which withdrew their milk, -
Ceremonially drunk amongst their ilk.
All their sheers then cut the hand that fed,
My limbs from their blood too ran red,
Till death greeted my corpse with a spasm…
Twice as joyous as this phantasm!

WE'LL BE BACK

The horizon beleaguers you,
Whilst I'm still pretending,
That my heart can't be ripped apart
By what it's contending...

And so you smile at your paradise,
Which you see impending -
But when I disappear, you'll learn
My love's never-ending.

A MUTTER FROM THE GUTTER

NORTH STAR

Though the crowd races onwards, I trail behind,
For I know the treasures ahead that they'll find,
And though I may never see or hold such things,
I'm contented with what your loving light brings.

While their eyes may never gaze upon the sky,
Your light I'll follow till the day that I die,
And if I am blinded by what is above,
Then I'd have been guided to the gifts of Love.

FROM RAGS TO REGICIDE

Though my gums bleed and teeth rot,
And I must share stale soap,
I swear an oath I will not
Become a misanthrope.
For, though every vermin's squeal
Distracts me from each rare meal,
Which opportune maggots steal,
I still retain some hope.

As some, their minds do harrow,
With endless wily schemes,
In hopes to clinch the marrow
Of everybody's dreams.
I too intend to enrich
Myself and soothe each itch;
I have hope in a coin, which
In my peasant palm gleams.

Triumph it does emanate,
My eyes with awe spiral,
Hoping I can emulate
Their posture so prideful,
And have people far and wide
Sing songs where I'm deified.
Oh, how could you be shocked I'd
Like to be my idol?

FROM RAGS TO REGICIDE

But if I'm to masquerade
As this splendid royal,
The riches I must parade
Of someone else's toil.
I must own robes all adore,
And palaces of grandeur,
Which I can flaunt to the poor
Whilst at them I recoil.

Oh, if it's my ambition,
To them, be more akin,
It must be a tradition
To gift my next of kin
All this wealth made from Man's woe,
Then those against the status quo,
We must ridicule as though
Their logic is a sin.

Yet, still my replication
Will not be just alike
If every other nation
With laughter doesn't strike,
As I bask in outlawry,
Placing with my hands so gory
England's supposed glory
To rot atop a pike.

THE DOCTOR SAID HE'S FINE

Left pale, his acouasm came in the sound of a choir,
The sun stared him in the face as he started to perspire,
Then tears fell down his face as he gazed into his pyre
Because the doctor said he's fine.

In the face of death, his palms were awfully sweaty,
He roared like a lion in the heart of the Serengeti,
As he stumbled and fell like he was made of spaghetti -
But the doctor said he's fine.

The doctor said he's fine,
And all his worries were dismissed,
But he falls down all the time,
Even when he isn't pissed.

The doctor said he's fine
(As he tried not to laugh).
It seems his practice is malign
Thanks to hypochondriacs.

The doctor said he's fine,
And to leave him alone;
He's tired of hearing him whine
In his silly trembled tone.

The doctor said he's fine,
And the doctor's never wrong.
You can hear his teeth grind
If he thinks you've stayed too long.

THE DOCTOR SAID HE'S FINE

The doctor said he's fine,
But you've heard all that before,
He dismissed all the signs
Then confirmed that he was sure.

Carefree, the yawning universe rose from their starry bed,
Their jaw opened up a synapse in a sickly head.
To spark the realization they'd soon be dead
Because the doctor said he's fine.

A LULLABY

Hush, my darling, it's time to sleep!
I will see if you try to peep!
Now to this world you must bid adieu,
For beyond nightfall's gates,
A world awaits that's just for you.
With lavender on your pillowcase,
Faraway, you will drift
To lands that grant your every wish -
Only if your eyelids do not lift
Till the sun casts its smile upon your face.

Hush, my darling, it's time to sleep!
I will see if you try to peep!
Your cheeks, pinker than a cherub's blush
Or hues in flowers of gardens plush,
As your dreams harmonise the hush,
Will smile at the moonbeams
As Wonder does appear
Upstream a distant place.
So hush, my darling, and do not fear
As I cast my smile upon your sleeping face.

TOOTHACHE

The torment did first begin
With devouring of sweet saccharine.
When those pleasures, rare and syrupy,
Became embedded in his cavity.
Those soft dainties, desires of his youth,
Agedly rankled his un-wizened tooth
With visions, filling him with scare,
Of his mouth agape on a dentist's chair;
His panicked mind could simply not prepare
For the mass inhalation of narcotic air.

He thought himself to not exist
(So needless would be a dentist)
But, incessantly, his pain further throbbed,
Whilst lamenting in vain, he further sobbed.
More tears rushed forth as his dream was killed
When reddened became the water he swilled.
Such sights, the curse, it would concoct
So that his festering tooth could further rot.
With mounting paleness, his sweat ran hot,
Learning his tooth's extraction could not be stopped...

But with the elapsing of time,
The dentist coaxed him to recline.
Pain, it lurked, his mind grew jittery -
Till pliers yanked the prize of victory:
An instant reversal of his glum frown;
The most bothersome, pearly, candied crown.
Now it all now seems so infantile
To have conjured up reasons to be hostile;
Now soothed, blessed, in jest, with a gapless smile,
He quips he won't be eating sweets for a while.

ANNE FRANK ON ACID

The sunrise watches over me as I stumble towards my
cigarettes,
Convinced they'll nurse my cough.
Today is but one day amongst a billion others that have been
and are yet to come -
But today is the day
I will explore new terrains. Yet, again, the unexpected is what I
expect.
The Earth may sink, the heavens may fall, the guns will shoot,
the animals will fuck but I will love, and I will live, and I will
hide.
I will hide in the hope that I can return to see the sun.
10:05 - kick-off.

Silence. How can such noise exist with such a cluttered mind?
The feet outside are trampling, the rain drops are crashing
Like they want to break inside!
Cats are meowing, birds are squawking, people talking.
Absolutely no peace of mind.
I press play and the objective experience withers;
Yes, I'm happy and alone
Yet accompanied by new sounds
That, with passion and newfound vision, crescendo into what is
to become
A brand new state of mind - this is what it has all been leading
up to.
Only a matter of time now.

ANNE FRANK ON ACID

11:21 - I have been catapulted through the catacombs of
cognition
Like a corkscrew winding deeper and deeper and deeper.
I didn't want to see those ghastly reptile eyes in the mirror
So I opted to instead reflect into further introspection.
I felt my head was made of wood and now it's as ripe as stone.
I just sit and listen and I wonder:
'Do the trampling feet have a place to go?
Do they run from the beauty of the rain
Or because they're scared of the consequences should they
mingle?'
If only there was a way I could be outside,
I could stop them,
I could show them,
They could see!
The animals aren't as blind as we think;
Their purrs resonate with allurement,
Rippling through the universe,
Singing and dancing with the fixtures of my ceiling.
I have a lucky feeling that today I'll see the sun!
The birds' tweets too are angelic,
Floating through the air, communicating somehow.
Why does everyone but I seem to ignore their passionate cries
So full of brio?
But, again, the dust jumps from behind the blinds
As my glimpses retreat back into their sobering shadow:
Why don't they know?
I'm not un-sure that I'm certain I know.
If
If only they knew!
11:22 - All you need is love.

ANNE FRANK ON ACID

The cygnet committee circled my thoughts,
They moved in synchronisation before they excelled.
Then they were a step ahead in everything I felt:
Making me try to manufacture a sun machine,
And paint my love upon a white balloon,
With rainbow skies in my beady eyes,
I was content to be alone on this journey,
Setting my sights closer to the sunshine -
In a different gear, yet still speeding.

But, now, I think for myself again.
My potential is fulfillable and my identity is malleable as long as
I am the leader of myself.
I swipe through the accompaniment to my aloneness;
My pictures. Or should I say vortexes?
I know what they are,
I've seen them billions of times before -
But they are as motionless as the clock which pretends to tick.
Then I remove my spectacles.
Dancing. They begin to dance in such a way that even
necrophilic worms,
Even nihilists, would be toe-tapping in their presence.
Jumping. Almost as though they are made of honeycomb and
have been concealing their treasure all along.
But now I see.
I see their kaleidoscopic cabaret performing and I have the
front and only seat, -
I witness green turn to red and red turn to purple,
Then purple start to dance!
I put my glasses back on and it all stops.
I have looking-glass eyes!

ANNE FRANK ON ACID

Next picture. Glasses off. The sun and the moon.
The moonlady is naked but I'm not seeking arousal.
She bites the apple and I pray for the crumbs of her
enlightenment.
Night and day combine,
The swirling unsettles my surroundings -
But then - I find myself in new lands;
Trapped inside the picture, I walk further from my creator,
Further from the artist,
Further from the sun.
Down arabesque avenues, I tumble and fall and search
Until a magician I meet, with many suns and moons on his
cloak.
I punch the air, hoping to rupture an exit -
There isn't one!
This is real!
As real as the room which drips around me.
"Do you believe in magic?" He half-said, half-sung, half-
squealed in such an un-familiar tongue,
Yet entirely comprehendible.
I was lost for words as translucent fishes turned fuchsia in my
eyeballs via neon-lighting,
And as the atmosphere exploded rivulets of my regrets down
my cheek,
Ganesh appeared in the holographic rain clouds momentarily -
But only to wave.
Then, - it was too late!
The spell was cast.

ANNE FRANK ON ACID

My legs began to itch,
My paws started to scratch,
And I ran against the tide of the whirlpool for a millennium,
Understanding not why Easter Island chased my tail,
Nor why the quicksands of Time were entrapping who I
thought I was,
Sinking deeper and deeper.
Trying my best not to trip on my laces,
I ran further and further into the maze
For thousands and thousands of years, through dictators, and
canals, and wars, and friendships -
Without any sign of the magician or an exit.
When I finally grew tired, I howled loudly at the moonlady.
Her dripping pussy edged tantalisingly closer.
I put my hand through the screen and changed the picture.
Home again.
My state of disbelief, believe it or not, was somewhat
underwhelming;
I had some more visual stimulation to be enticed by -
This time, it was a crystal temple with commensurate pillars.

ANNE FRANK ON ACID

By this point, I was really cooking,
So, again, they jived - but with rapid intensity,
With colours more prominent,
Movement with more pizazz!
Until I realised, from it was emanating a hum.
A static feel seemed to brush against my nose,
I saw that I was about to vanish,
I hoped I'd at last get to see the sun!
Closer and closer I moved,
All the while, the music played.
I felt less and less alone;
My smile beamed
But there was no-one else around.
No, not even the sun.
The time is 12:47.

1:53pm - I'm no longer alone.
My brother, the bedlamite, has been taken on an outing.
Sobriety and excitement I feign, -
Both go undetected.
Does he remember what happened?
Has he changed?
I can't quite tell if it's because he's melting or if the pills are
making him gain weight.
I hope he's okay -
But those almond eyes! Those dark, satanic almond eyes!
His vacant stare! I can tell he still isn't there.
Today of all days...
How has this managed to happen?
How am I supposed to act?

ANNE FRANK ON ACID

My heart is beating like a wakeful lion,
My passions are roaring 'I love you'.
That's all I have ever wanted to tell him
But etiquette and awkwardness may never allow me, -
And I want him to feel it!
In this moment, the only reason I am living is for him to hear
these words -
But his ears are as restless as seashells clogged with emptiness.
I wonder if he wants to stab me still.
I remember those words so vividly,
I remember all his glossolalic babbling before the doctor took
him away,
His plan to bury me in the garden next to the cat,
And I have a memory from our childhood of him pushing my
pram,
Looking over me and swearing an oath to protect me with his
eyes
Before we'd ever drew blood from one another -
And it was beautiful.
But I can't forget that day. I can't forget the tales of him butting
the nurses,
Of them holding him down,
Of them sedating him.
I wonder how such a thing must have felt for him.
I wonder if he still remembers me at all!

ANNE FRANK ON ACID

Telepathically, I tell him:
"Brother, I come in peace!
Let it be known that I wish nothing but the best for you,
Even if that meant that we'd be stuck inside all day,
Never to see daylight, nor the sun.
I want you to know that I love you,
Not the devil which lies behind you,
But what the devil's scared to face.
Yes, I am convinced you've been possessed
Long ago by those crocodile-cunts,
Hanging from the clothesline, in their suits - invisible to the rest
of us.
But, before I break the ouija boards out,
Allow my words to move your soul
Out from the darkness
Into redemption;
See my smiling yellow teeth,
See how everything about you makes me want to cry -
And know that I will not taste my blood tonight!"
He just looked at me, empty.
My mother then led him hand-by-hand for a day trip to the park
Which reminded me of a child I once knew.
Everything happened so fast.

Upstairs, to feathers I float.
Now I'm hiding from the apocalyptic sun!
Now I'm watching the never-ending wheels!
The time is meaningless.
The time is just an invention
I think...
But it's also 3:45 now.
He's just left.
Back to the hospital,
I wonder, back to peace?
How time flies!
Who knows what will happen next?

ANNE FRANK ON ACID

5:44pm - I do.
I am the soothsayer!
I witnessed the nails close Huxley's coffin,
I took a bite from Leary's muffin,
And found that for the truth I'm still starving!
The bullets and bombs surrounded me from all angles and dimensions,
From my family and from the neighbours,
In the open and in secrecy,
And I found that, perhaps, I was selfish;
Yearning to be alone, yearning for a little spot of sunlight
So that I don't feel forever trapped inside,
So that I can scream from the rooftops:

"What the fuck does anyone know about anything?
What the fuck do you think you'll learn if you can't even believe this is
possible?
What the fuck am I supposed to believe?
How did we even end up here?"
And have my echo reply harmoniously over harmoniums and sitars
With a double-tracked vocal, "Nothing at all, now shine on you crazy
diamond!"
But, for now, all I can hear is those high-flying birds,
Soaring over my head,
Caught in the midst of a thunderstorm,
And I am bamboozled as to what they have learned from all their
experience.
Apparently, it is nothing.
Let them fly until tomorrow!
Until tomorrow never comes!
Whoa!
Just sneezed and it felt like a brand new sensation.
I think the moonlady may have another strike,
Maybe even bestow me with an OBE for all my loyalty -
My fingers will be crossed!
9:19pm - full-time.

MONEYSHAKERS

Won't you try some honey, won't you try some honey,
Lose your mind and lose your money
Down avenues of cornucopic vice.
Oh, just be enticed - and try some honey,
Which flows like a freshet's unexpected flood
Upon your every eager bud.

Won't you buy some honey, won't you buy some honey,
Lose your mind and lose your money.
Its viscid touch will have your heart caught.
Oh, you really ought to buy some honey
From whose tender lips will devour
From morning rise to midnight-hour.

You'll soon be trying, then be buying,
To see Heaven stretched above you, lying
Smothered with ravishing runny,
Pure nectarous, fulsome, and lickerish honey,
Sucked from the unwonted flower
Which rises at the midnight-hour.

THE WITCH HUNT

The night sky and dim clouds converse
Through their whispering utters
Whilst moonlit bats, in swarms traverse,
With their muffled flutters
Over silent, dead boughs,
By which, a man does rouse
To life his whole town,
Serving up The Tavern's brown.

As music plays, and tankards clink,
A drunkard tells a joke.
Forcing some to choke on their drink,
Then focus on my croak, -
Which emanates from me
In fits of ecstasy,
Blissfully unaware
Of their suspicious glare.

With my green-skin, hook-nose, and hat,
I try to clarify -
But, before I get a chance for that,
I hear someone shrilly cry:
"Burn the witch, and drown their ash!"
Then their teeth duly gnash
As they start to revolt
And, for my life, I bolt.

THE WITCH HUNT

Rumours spread over brooks and glens
From the mouths of guileful press,
Which expose my family and friends'
Cold, sheepish fickleness;
Questioning my sick mind
Rather than the truth find,
And end up by my side -
Whilst mulling suicide.

My heart quickens, as do my feet,
With every single sound.
Till I think it could be bittersweet
If I was finally found.
Suddenly, my mouth is gagged,
And to a stake I'm dragged,
Then by their torches,
My green-skin slowly scorches.

Beneath the crackling, swelling flames,
They dance in revelry.
As nothing of myself remains -
Thus nor my deviltry.
So I can never reveal
To those whom saw me squeal,
Watch me die, then smiled, -
That I was just a child.

THE CROWD'S SINGING PROUD

The Sun's castaway shadow cannot hide
From the effulgent procession of your pride,
Sung like a restless alleluiatic choir
To lift us to dreams from which we'll never tire.

Though, outwardly, death appears dark and long,
The cosmos, it's unable to bedim;
Just to hear a lyric or note of your song -
Will resuscitate everything within.

GLASS HALF-SPIKED

ALL ROADS LEAD TO YOU

Let this bachelor's kingdom be besieged -
His metropolis has grown malnourished!
However spectacular seems the crown,
The heritors may keep it, for my queen
Has fled - but I still remain encouraged,
Someday, we'll encounter beyond this town.

All roads lead to you
But what will lead you to me?
Will all of my love help you see?
All roads lead to you,
Always here I will be.

Afar, deep in the regal wilderness
Whilst dying in the shady, sylvan glade,
I see her face in every dewdrop's gleam,
And she is proud that I'm now silverless.
Then, my heart quickens and all colours fade
As my dulcinea wakes me from this dream.

All roads lead to you
But what will lead you to me?
Will all of my love help you see?
All roads lead to you,
Always here I will be.

ALL ROADS LEAD TO YOU

I chase her through arabesque alleyways.
Lovesick with her devilish enchantment.
I spend my entire life and my pocket,
Wallowing in memories of her gaze,
Hoping she'll retrieve her missing fragment
From my hands to fit her broken locket.

All roads lead to you
But what will lead you to me?
Will all of my love help you see?
All roads lead to you,
Always here I will be.
All roads lead to you,
Do you see?

THE RAVEN (AND THE SKYLARKS)

To naked eyes, magically magnets gather -
But what apparatus explains the cadent chime,
Which allures me to cavort afoot that tyrant, Time,
A dance, which to all else, sounds like rhythmic blather?

Forever ponderous is the furrowed mask of Fate;
He who is not aware of how, or why, or when
The time will come when Heaven's hand hoists him a pen
From billows of clouds for his dreams to consummate.

Such mysteries, in the warmth of my breath behold,
Until they reveal like mist in the speechless cold
And rest beyond zeniths where wings can't stretch to fly;

No amount of gold could pay a mystic to see
The ear to the tuneful ear, the eye of sightly eye, -
Nor the voice that is the force of my destiny.

I'VE NEVER EVEN BIT A SPIDER

Incy Wincy, fuck you!
Why must you crawl beneath my shoe,
And fill my loving heart with guilt
As from your masterpiece ghosts hang
Who glimpse my frightful fang
From which your Earthly ink was spilt?

UP, UP, UP AND FAR, FAR AWAY

You cannot care for any care
If your figments lead you astray
To be anywhere anywhere
And emblazon your ashen day
Up, up, up and far, far away.

Be whatever you want to be,
Say what it is you need to say.
See in the light you wish to see
A universe in every ray,
A universe in every ray.

Down, down, down where blind lead the blind,
Down, down, down where blind lead the blind,
Down on your knees you cry and pray
That, somehow, somewhere you will find
A way to shift the clouds of grey.

But all you need to do is breathe,
Breathe life into the breathless clay,
And believe that when you believe
They'll find themselves a place to play
Up, up, up and far, far away.

VANILLA ESSENCE

Perfume of vanilla essence,
Sightless with its evanescence,
Falls gently, then on lovers shows, -
The gateway to the heart's the nose.

The face of Love, you truly see,
With such sweet scented-filigree;
You'll see as her cheeks blush to rose,
The gateway to her heart's the nose.

All of my senses disappear,
But my heart beats when she walks near.
Thus, fleeting fragrances expose,
The gateway to my heart's the nose.

Perfume of vanilla essence,
Forever linger in my nose!

BALLAD OF THE BEES

Loop-the-looping eternally,
A symphony to seize
The mind with its monotony;
The ballad of the bees.

With virgin eyes scouring above
Lush and learned flowers.
Appreciating godly art,
He hovered there for hours,

Feeling it was his destiny
To be a collector,
He occupied the afternoon
Guzzling their sweet nectar.

Loop-the-looping eternally,
A symphony to seize
The mind with its monotony;
The ballad of the bees.

While he lay vigil, with new sights,
Horizons expanded.
He noticed, filled with ecstasy,
Earthbound he was stranded.

Meanwhile, with vacancy he stared
Deep into his future,
Marooned atop a velvet bed
By his greedy stupor.

BALLAD OF THE BEES

Loop-the-looping eternally,
A symphony to seize
The mind with its monotony;
The ballad of the bees.

His blaring buzz caused vexation
As his senses sharpened;
As the abyss filled him with smite,
His eyes further darkened.

To deluge it with his babbling
Was his preferred resort -
But the truthful revelations
He just could not distort.

Loop-the-looping eternally,
A symphony to seize
The mind with its monotony;
The ballad of the bees.

The champion of extraction,
Himself, he did proclaim,
And with that injurious lie
His knees, he clutched, in pain.

He firmly remained impassioned
About his delusion,
And cursed every drop of honey
Tasted by a human.

BALLAD OF THE BEES

Loop-the-looping eternally,
A symphony to seize
The mind with its monotony;
The ballad of the bees.

From the flowers he ascended,
Thinking his job was done.
Though he'd conquered their sugared lands,
Their love he never won.

Aimless and bloodshot were his sights
Due to the endless ring;
Whispers trying to convince him
To weaponize his sting.

Loop-the-looping eternally,
A symphony to seize
The mind with its monotony;
The ballad of the bees.

But before sunup awoke him,
Whilst in his homely hive,
Where his father's abusiveness
Inspired him to strive

To flaunt his inner emptiness,
Which left eyebrows unraised,
But now pollen did run through him, -
All saw that he was crazed.

BALLAD OF THE BEES

Loop-the-looping eternally,
A symphony to seize
The mind with its monotony;
The ballad of the bees.

His lips freshly shimmered
As sweetness crystallised, -
But with his buzzing grew a fear
Which then somaticized:

His ears were clogged, and he derobed
Himself and made a crown;
His ambition spawned potential
But his sting weighed him down.

Loop-the-looping eternally,
A symphony to seize
The mind with its monotony;
The ballad of the bees.

Then by evermore vicious thoughts,
He found himself possessed,
As all notions of consequence
Had packed their bags and left.

Inwardly, he was reminded
Of everything he lacked,
And when a human approached him,
He outwardly attacked.

BALLAD OF THE BEES

Loop-the-looping eternally,
A symphony to seize
The mind with its monotony;
The ballad of the bees.

He penetrated his poison
To cause a measly prick.
Soon after, alone and mindless,
He began to grow sick.

As he lay dying without pride,
He pondered his own birth.
In death, he figured out the price
Of what sweetness is worth.

Loop-the-looping eternally,
A symphony to seize
The mind with its monotony;
The ballad of the bees.

Still, bees continue with their lives,
Suckling heavenly spores.
Carefree, they engorge the honey
That opulently pours.

The flowers maintain their beauty
To all their clientele
In the place where they stand up proud -
Where one poor bastard knell.

BALLAD OF THE BEES

Loop-the-looping eternally,
A symphony to seize
The mind with its monotony;
The ballad of the bees.

INTERPRETING A BUTTERFLY

I think, whilst wrapped in silk cocoon
'From this change, one can't be immune:
One must surrender to the croon
Sung by the moon, sung by the moon'.

I close my eyes and life springs forth,
The sky I see as I look north.
Did I create the world before?
It's just a thought, it's just a thought.

My thoughts come from a different brain,
My new heart, it beats, just the same.
How do I still feel love and pain?
I can't explain, I can't explain.

My disbelief, it has me torn:
Can what one creates freely swarm?
Or everything since they were born
Must I perform, must I perform?

Unknown knowledge falls from the sky,
Un-mimicked sights seduce the eye.
Then suddenly, I wonder why
I can now fly, I can now fly.

Meanwhile, the passing of the moon
Has broken light on my cocoon.
With winglessness, it hangs immune
In my bedroom, in my bedroom.

PARADISE

To B.W.Z. Oiller

From eternity, we can never leave.
Though we may drift far from the chersonese,
Forever anchored, shall rest our memories.

But, for eternity, your wits I could admire,
From your quips, my ears could never tire,
My long-living, prosperous, noble squire.

No plaintive anthem need be sung
To ascend higher up a heavenly rung:

No yearning for yesteryear, however fond,
Could ever break our immortal bond.

With you, there's no other for who I'd pine
For no one's company is quite as divine!
How you further sweeten the finest wine,
And how you ever enhance the most heartiest vibe
When, in your magic, I do imbibe.

As I try to pluck what's beyond the clouds above,
I find, ineffable are the words of love
But - for you, this toilsome trek I'll bravely trudge,
Though I'll still too express it with a nudge:
As your fervid fire mellows this world of ice,
Plashless rest these tears from the eyes of Paradise.

A CONFORMIST'S SCRAPBOOK

POMPEII

Pondering Nature's construction
Beholds my eyes to see
Its potential for destruction,
And see itself in me.
How forever I am studious
Of how your greatness shakes the ground -
Yet, dear Mount Vesuvius,
To your shadow I am bound.

As I witness the abysm,
I'm made to feel unwise;
Choking midst the cataclysm
As blackness fills the skies.
Ejecta tumbles, creating tombs
For those whom your lava maimed.
Oh beloved town, victim of Doom,
What of you will remain?

As somehow my mind remembers
Everything in my past,
Phoenixlike, I rise from embers
And see beneath me cast:
All of my friends stood together,
Each disfigured, and charred.
As I am struck with displeasure,
Their memory is marred...

POMPEII

Motionless, with immunity
To ever-morphing Time,
Together, they watch gloomily
The stars of crystalline
Flicker nightly, far out of reach
From their daydreaming doze;
Oh, how the future looks so bleak
When in history you're froze.

To my chagrin, I discover
Through their eyes I'm scalded.
Like them, I am just another
Lifeless corpse re-moulded;
Despite my ashes scattering,
Who they think of as Me
Is naught but an unflattering
And distant memory.

No, I am not the same as you,
Who I was, I did raze,
And you'll too be gone when I spew
My great infernal blaze.
Stay ignorant of my hissing,
I couldn't give a damn;
When I shake the world, the world will listen
And know who I really am.

THE VILLAGE IDIOT

Ostracised, they all point and laugh -
But I don't have a choice;
I'm unable to walk their path
And pretend to rejoice,
Whilst willingly my Potential,
From its dreams, I omit.
So I'm known for being mental:
The village idiot.

So I'm known for being mental:
The village idiot.

Intellect in a braindead world
Is inutile and so
Abuse at me is always hurled
Everywhere that I go.
Shockingly, it's seen as good
To be illiterate,
Whereas I am seen as deadwood;
The village idiot.

Whereas I am seen as deadwood;
The village idiot.

All menial labour is viewed
A noble ambition;
To jostle midst the multitude
For that's the tradition -
And so me too, to my dismay,
They attempt to conscript
But I'm he who walks the other way;
The village idiot.

THE VILLAGE IDIOT

I'm he who walks the other way;
The village idiot.

By deviating from the norm
One spawns innovation,
So if everyone did conform
Where'd come our creation?
With this in mind, you'd expect them
To be considerate
But instead they choose to condemn
The village idiot.

But instead they choose to condemn
The village idiot.

Still, they remain ignorant to
The Artist's genocide.
Despite all that I try to do,
They can't be edified.
Oh, how they would love to defame
Everything I have writ
So, with pitiless stares, they do maim
The village idiot.

With pitiless stares, they do maim
The village idiot.

I KNOW NOTHING

Assumptions broke the camel's back,
I know nothing - and that's a fact!
But still, I hear outlandish claims,
Thoughts, supposedly, from their brains.
Which, before I became aware,
Those same beliefs I once did share.
Before I questioned everything,
Assumptions even I did sing -
But now I'm sure I've seen the light,
I understand what's wrong and right,
Such sureties, I'll now confess:
I know nothing... thus they know less.

JUST ANOTHER GRAIN TO THE SANDSTORM

If your head's out the sand, get up off your knees,
The time's nigh for you to transform.
If you don't move you'll be blown away, so please
Follow me and you'll be reborn.
If in the power of Change you don't believe,
You're just another grain to the sandstorm.

If the solutions to problems are found with ease,
Why then of hope are you forlorn?
If you don't want to know what the blind man sees,
Move as the flecks begin to swarm.
If in the power of Change you don't believe,
You're just another grain to the sandstorm.

If your blistering brain does not feel unease
At how this world we could adorn,
As you are pushed along by the gentlest breeze,
Beyond the dunes, your soul I'll mourn;
If in the power of Change you don't believe,
You're just another grain to the sandstorm.
Oh, you're just another grain to the sandstorm.

MANTRA OF A MANNEQUIN

They repeat the lies they invent
So, in your mind, they will indent
Some mental memoranda.
Then the puppeteers will deceive
As, spiral-eyed you will believe,
Naively, propaganda.

ACTUALLY, I'M A NAME NOT A NUMBER

Greeted with a countenance most downcast,
Your life ahead they cheerily present,
To which, you must be an enthusiast
Or have them your inborn freedom resent,
Resulting from their gloomy discontent,
And you must by gales of guilt be terrorised
In the hope that they can dissuade dissent,
Till you're inspired by whom you are advised,
To heroically become like them; dehumanised...

But don't be misguided by their malice
As your death won't be cared for by the dead.
Don't be dispirited by words callous
Nor let your destiny by them be led
To see your sepulchre a comfy bed;
Be the storm that shakes them from their slumber,
And awake yourself from their dreams of dread
With words so loud that you quake their thunder,
"Actually, I'm a name not a number."

PARADIGM SHIFT

Dear Wanderer, seeking the Absolute,
Blind to the constellations most immense,
Led down corridors of Coincidence
To find purpose in your perennial pursuit,
With intention to Her origins uproot
At your defiant featherweight heart's expense.
Know, to the eye, the mystery's so dense -
And, thence, you won't will such a fact to transmute.

But wander onwards with your wayward mind,
Till you're afoot Imagination's gates
And notice how, out of nothing, it creates
An entire kingdom made from within.
It's in this darkness that Her love you'll find
To transform your heart to see real change begin.

THE RAT RACE

Not a living man today did pave
The path so many have dared to brave,
Now I must too walk towards my grave
In silence of being a dead man's slave.

Traipsing gutters, damp and wet,
I am drenched by beads of sweat,
Which fall like teardrops of my pain -
Helping hide my eyes' disdain.

Meanwhile, my crestfallen brain
Dreams of a lobotomy,
In hope this monotony
Will someday see the end
So this world I can transcend -

But I can't argue with Fate,
(For doing so, may make me late!)
So, as with quickened steps I walk,
I hear a spectral stalker stalk.

They chase me down each avenue,
Like a puppeteer to all I do,
Till my every step they have led -
As I'm afraid to turn my head.

Each time my foot hits the ground,
Petrified, my heart does pound,
As like my shadow they cling tight,
Cimmerian as a starless night.

THE RAT RACE

This chase I'm not thrilled to survive,
When at my job I arrive,
And my morale plummets even more
As I see Death within each chore;

I adhere to absurd demands
With sweaty palms and calloused hands,
And as I acquire each burn and scar
I hear them laughing from afar.

Their teeth like headstones clang and grind,
And ricochet inside my mind,
Whilst I wince at each macabre smell,
Which to them, are just perfumes of Hell.

I strain each and every muscle,
Against the clock, I must hustle,
And I'm thanked for this effete work
With only their pallid smirk,

Which haunts my periphery,
As my boss adds to my misery,
Reminding me I'm under control
Of no-one but his rayless soul.

He stands grotesque and corpulent,
And onto me he does vent,
His frustration with this savage world,
In which he feels he too was hurled.

Then, myself I do not defend,
Instead, I smile and pretend
That, though we were both born equally,
Somehow he's now worth more than me,

THE RAT RACE

And I feign that I do not see
Death whispering in his ear,
That pernicious puppeteer,
Telling him just what to say
To wreak more havoc on my day.

Eventually, I can leave
And my integrity start to grieve
Which sits, as homewards I return,
In me, like ashes in an urn -

But now, every bus and train
Appears to my tiny brain,
Like a boat upon the waves
To transport the herds of slaves,

And with every clank and rattle,
Here we sit, just like cattle,
Waiting for our time to kill
With no belief in our free-will

Till a putrid stench hits my nose
And I see their flesh decompose,
To reveal their brittle skeleton
And fill me with adrenaline.

Then onto my road I stride,
With a familiar foe by my side,
Whose rimy breath chills each bone
I use to hasten towards my home.

THE RAT RACE

His every move does terrify
But I let out a solaced sigh,
As the door slams to end the chase
Right in his unsightly face.

Some sovereignty I retrieve
When I return every eve,
And my TV flickers in my eyes
And some of my stress does tranquillise,

And absinthe makes my heart grow fonder
With what cash I can squander,
Using it to self-medicate
The illness that's my waking-state.

But neither of these pleasures still
Can a void inside fulfil;
My urge to grant a gift to Earth
Which I feel its beauty's worth.

I hear him tapping my window pane -
But there's little more fright he can drain.
I see his face on the ale I drink -
But I don't have time to think.

I just sit and let him speak to me
Through the actors on my TV.
Then, together, we both grin
Listening to demonic din

Till my attention does divert
In the middle of an advert,
Selling coffins to the old and ripe,
Or life insurance, or other tripe,

THE RAT RACE

For how glorious looks my bed,
Where wearily falls my head,
Where I can bury all my sorrow
Till I wake up on the morrow.

Then roosters crow, morning breaks,
And my slumbersome mind awakes
To again greet my routine -
And live out someone else's dream.

Again, towards my job I walk.
Again, I hear Death's footsteps stalk,
And louder is his chilling rasp
Each time my leg he tries to grasp.

Wherever I go, he lingers,
Outstretching his decrepit fingers,
Circling me down every path
In hope that I will feel his wrath, -

And I am, to such distress,
Simply rendered powerless.
With just one thing not to be downbeat, -
The myth I'm told I must repeat,

That vicious repetitious lie,
That extending into the sky
Is a ladder I can ascend
That will bring the chase to an end.

Which, perhaps if I do not think,
That Time and Death do interlink,
Manifesting in all I do,
Perhaps I could pretend it's true...

THE RAT RACE

But I see as each rung I climb,
A glimpse of Death mowing Time,
Cutting seconds like blades of grass
Till, before I know, years do pass,

And still just at his thought I writhe,
Climbing from his glaring scythe,
Till I turn pale from his touch
As my very heart he does clutch.

He drags me by it and I fall
Helplessly towards my pall,
And I spiral down, not from the top,
Yet still endlessly seem to drop

Till I eventually strike the ground
And whimper with a dying sound.
Then, suddenly, I see left
My body of its life bereft

As I float up high above
To the welcoming light of Love,
Far away from the tears of woe
So opulent in the world below.

Then, 'neath their incorporeal wing,
Which permeates everything,
I'm told that here I must stay
And watch my entire life replay.

First I see something I'd forgot:
How they'd lay with me in my cot,
And softly lullabies they'd sing
Of how the future's so promising,

THE RAT RACE

And in hide and seek as a child,
Or amongst Nature, running wild,
Sweet Love was always by my side -
Till soon they'd seek whilst I would hide,

As next I see I was mandated
Into a system most outdated;
Where for questions they'd no concern -
In where I'd been told I'd come to learn,

And Love's whisperings I could hear
As inquisitiveness in my ear -
But, to them, blind diligence
To what they'd say was intelligence

So when I'd ask, like militants,
In a chorus they would bleat:
'All that you're told you must repeat
And not a word you shall protest -
Unless you want to fail the test!'

Then from institute to institute,
With the multitude I did commute,
And I see from Love we did proceed
To run from in a great stampede.

I watch as adults were bewildered
To accept slavery when it's gilded
With the promise of being paid, -
Dependant upon how well they grade.

THE RAT RACE

For how much money they possess
They've been told equates to success
By all in authority and Fame -
Not that they'll starve if they leave the game,

Nor that the poor and unemployed
With the same dreams, aren't overjoyed,
And thus in the name of getting gold -
Crime and murders grow manifold,

Whilst rich men are dissatisfied
In the mansions where they reside,
And some inheriting for free
So much wealth they'll never spend or see, -

And I notice how both rich and poor,
The masses would not deplore,
For each action, to some degree,
They could relate some sympathy -

But when someone did voice a doubt,
Collectively, they'd be drown out, -
As they'd take the upmost offence
At someone's disobedience.

For it took their envy to the brink,
As their misery made them think,
If jobs they work, then you must too:
Jobs no-one wants nor has to do.

Then I see how I did heed their word
And continued following the herd;
Discarding all our aspirations
Just to profit corporations

THE RAT RACE

Till, eventually, we are the dead.
I see everyone on their deathbed
Who shed all their blood and sweat -
And every one's full of regret, -

And I see in my aged eye,
Tears of regret I also cry,
As Death, my existence smothers
Like the billions of others,

And I see with every tear cried,
Love sits by each bedside,
And was with us every single day
Hoping we'd come out to play.

Then my vision's consumed with dark,
From the radiant realm I disembark,
And my illumined soul which does glance
Incarnates to grant me one more chance.

Now, the material, I'm aware
Is just a finespun gossamer,
Aware of its visibility -
But also its fragility.

Not a living man today did pave
The path so many have dared to brave,
So why would I walk towards my grave
In silence of being a dead man's slave?

I am Love, and Love is free
To be anything there can be.
So if I choose to raise my voice
My free-will allows for such a choice.

THE RAT RACE

So hear me loud and hear me clear
Death, you fill me with no fear,
For we are Love, and we are free
To be anything we want to be, -

And if in your heart you agree,
Someone this world must start anew -
Well, if not us, then tell me who,
And if the time is not now, then
Please tell me exactly when.

Every gift there is to give
From anyone on this rock we live
We don't longer have to thwart
We can embrace them and support.

For anyone who can see the end,
Their perceptions will transcend,
As from cocoons emerge butterflies,
And flowers from the muck do rise.

So with courage and not cowardice,
Before opportunities are missed;
Before you leave this beautiful Earth
Express what you feel your life is worth, -

And Death and Time may well still loom,
And escort you to your tomb,
But take their power from your pyre
By using its vision to inspire,

THE RAT RACE

And in yourself, truly believe,
Beyond the last breath you breathe,
And listen to your soul that does glow,
Telling you what you already know:

'Yes, please know that you're not alone,
That in life Death we can dethrone,
For we are Love, and we are free
To be anything we want to be, -

And if in your heart you agree,
Someone this world must start anew -
Well, if not us, then tell me who,
And if the time is not now, then
Please tell me *exactly* when'.

GRIEVANCES FOR THE LIVING

STRUCK BY LIGHTNING

Out the blue you graced this world, and my heart,
With zap and whisperings so thunderous,
Before my hiding place you tore apart
And exposed me to your sparks most wondrous.
Igniting palpitations from this fate,
At which the skeptics look at me askance;
Questioning where Love does originate
And if our souls met by more than mere chance.
As when I saw you emerge from the sky,
When angel-like, rising from clouds you struck,
No-one could shield a purpose from my eye
Or convince me that you were my bad luck.
For despite all of your chaotic wrath,
Heaven sent you to guide me to your path.

SPRING IS ALIVE TODAY

Walk this way! Oh, walk this way!
See how Spring is alive today!
Tread through here! Oh, tread through here -
The garland heartland of each year.
Hear it beat! Oh, hear it beat!
See blossom swaying with your feet
But know, what does bloom must retreat
Just like sweet yesterday.

Oh, blessed Spring! Blessed Spring!
I wish birds could forever sing
Sweet soulful songs 'neath skies of blue;
Odes to flowers, brimful with hue -
But Time's their cataractal eye
As death is near, death is nigh.

Walk this way! Oh, walk this way!
See how Spring is alive today!
But do not trip! Oh, do not fall -
Or through Winter's past you must crawl,
And in the end, do not blink,
Though the sun's rays may make you wince
For all its beauty, you must glimpse -
Since Spring is alive today.

ODDITIES

We were mesmerized by Love's kaleidoscopic beauty
But the light made us blind before we saw the spectrum.
Now I'm compelled into feeling it's my divine duty
To suffer just to garner your affection;
I don't want a post-structuralist apocalypse,
Nor the matriarchies, of which, you're so keen
But, darling, I know if I'm again to kiss your lips,
I mustn't let my logic intervene...

And though it may be true our souls aren't simpatico;
That your cynicism's at war with my hope for peace,
That it's impossible to know how to react apropos
In the face of your mindless, clockworklike caprice.
If you relinquished your grip and told me I'm free,
In your cell I'll stand unmoved with unshackled feet,
For it's in Love's imperfect shadow that I see,
Without you in my life I'm incomplete.

AN ALBATROSS IN WAITING

I wonder what sights you have seen,
As I wait here, longing for you.
Is an ocean enough to come between
The vast piquant enchantment of us two?
Or will one's suavity act as a lure
To capture your rutilant yearned-for face?
I won't move till we're on the shore,
Reuniting with an embrace,
Till your rubicund lips are in view,
Till, instead of one body, they're on two -
But, - till then, I'll just wait for you.

My pupils do dilate for you
So you can stare into my soul.
With amativeness, me, you do imbue
When we're together, making me feel whole.
Your mind is pearlsome enough to marry,
Your voice caresses my soul that quivers.
For you, my love, I shall tarry
Until my skeleton withers!
Forgive my tearfulness on your adieu
And please, before my heartache does imbue,
Remember that I'll wait for you.

Once again, I'm wondering
As my triphammer heart beats,
Whether you're aware of its thundering
As the cruel cycle of longing repeats.
Do I possess enough magnetism
To influence your compass and make you return?
And despite all of our repetition
Do you think someday that, together, we will learn?
Honey, I don't mind not having a clue
How many miles our little minds have flew -
I'll still be waiting here for you.

I PICKED IT JUST FOR YOU

My dotingness inspires me to explain
All the ways you won't be told you're unique,
And though my captivation shall not wane,
Some fail to see glamour in your mystique.
Their psychotic senselessness, don't bewail;
Like no other, you trapped my love perchance,
And my death's release, will leave you a trail
Of petals to an eyesome amaranth.
Though its beauty permeates everywhere,
Don't forget where to look when I depart;
Don't keep it hidden in a jardiniere,
Forever keep it treasured in your heart,
So when elysian eyes shed their dew,
Hear me whisper: "I picked it just for you".

DEAD FLOWERS

When I bestow you with a gift,
It leaves you looking rather miffed,
For their severed heads are topped with blood,
And they're not grounded like they should.

I notice how your eyes do shift,
When I bestow you with a gift,
As you see that their backs are arched,
And notice that their lips are parched.

As their petals droop - and you wince,
I must confess, that I'm convinced,
When I bestow you with a gift
My body from this world could drift.

I wonder if your looks could kill,
They'd sit atop your windowsill,
Pondering if their lives are missed
When I bestow you with a gift.

CAN I PUT THIS IN A POEM?

Forgive all my mind's lechery
As our hearts beat with ecstasy,
And my lips press against your skin
Whilst brimful with adrenaline.
No, of me, don't think any less
If your silken thighs I caress,
As my lust, to you, I endear
With gentle nibbles of your ear.

Your degrees of how amorous
Waver with what's deemed glamorous -
But allow me to lift this veil,
Surrender bliss with each exhale,
And rejoice that each teasing breath
Ascend like whispers into Death.

My tongue helplessly can't neglect
Your pert nipples, which stand erect,
Whilst my hair with vigour you clutch,
As your wetness my fingers touch.
No longer acting as if chaste,
Excitedly, you have a taste.
Now you've succumb to thoughts so lewd,
More than your veil I can denude.

I love it how you roll your eyes
As my head's lodged betwixt your thighs,
And all of your moans I adore,
Moans from my tireless tongue and jaw -
And from such chivalry you'll learn
To grant your curtsy in return.

CAN I PUT THIS IN A POEM?

Once you've gladly worshipped and bowed
Before this gift I was endowed,
And seen it throb just at the thought
Of being sheathed by your wet taut
Pussy that's feverishly hot -
Let it reach its inmost spot,
And intermingle through the night
As both our lips you try to bite.

Tell me I still seem debonair,
As with a fistful of your hair,
I spank your ass over my bed
Till its peachiness turns to red,
And you let out a fervent shriek
As each thrust makes your knees go weak.

With your final enraptured scream,
In my eye you will see a gleam
That knows you would like me to share
What you long to drip everywhere, -
And so zestfully you'll obey,
For despite what all your friends say,
I think you know I can't degrade
Someone who wants to be enslaved.

Once you swallow every last drop,
Our racing hearts come to a stop
And our passional selves perish -
Yet still we can't help but cherish
An orgasm's intrinsic joy,
Whilst pretending we're creatures coy.

RELAPSES FROM REHAB

With brute naivete, cursing Cupid's aim
And his lazy eye, I had misunderstood
That not Providence, nor man's wired mortal brain
Could find a way to attract me like you could,
And levitate me to reach Paradise
With dulcet notes you use to entice,
And gambol further with your velvet hand
Whilst a heavenly band
Of harpists gracefully pluck melodies
To accompany our impassioned dance,
As over motley auroras we prance,
Like we're escaping the prison of Time
After being held captive for no crime, -
And there, I kiss lips that exuviate my skin,
Then! A nauseating spin!
Smothering of vibrant skies!
And the demon who's behind the eclipse
Roars with laughter at the poison on my lips,
As the instruments make discordant whines -
I see only the waning of what shines,
And I shiver, I freeze whilst all alone,
And your bewitching beauty I bemoan,
Crying at the thought of losing a good friend
With no-one to witness my tears or my blood
That fall in solitude as the urge I wrest
To press my dying ear against your pounding breast.

IS IT REALLY OVER?

In the terminal, I see teardrops well,
I see memories mourn their existence -
And posthumously long for life. I see
All this in the reflection of your eyes.

Now that sightlessness has swept over me,
Rekindling love's all I can envisage -
But your kiss, that ever-ebbing image,
With voodoo, haunts my lips eternally.

Perhaps those words of mine will one day haunt you
Via delicate whispering in your ear;
Perhaps we'll ponder what constitutes the end.

In your hands is my bloodied, beating heart,
But the vision in each our eyes is clear
As we walk, together, towards the start.

AFTERWORD

AFTERWORD

I have discovered that writing a book tends to encompass a trinity of books; the book you plan to write, the book you write, and the book you edit.

As the cover was hand drawn, the numbers were hand placed, and the self-proclaimed millionaire saviours of the self-published were of course basking in extortion, I felt it would be worth re-editing this book five years on from its original release in 2016 to share it with the world in a format which I feel its contents is deserving.

Not because I'm a masochist that's aroused by the embarrassment of people seeing work I now consider to be juvenilia, because I think it is important for my readership to come on the journey of my writing career rather than have my development be as mysterious as Shakespeare's by putting a flame to it instead and have its ashes drift into the wastelands of obscurity; I began writing the book having never read a collection of poems in my life and ended it as a poet.

My ambition is not only to demystify but to also have this work be appreciated for the handful of gems and mysteries within it, becoming the conversation piece it was originally designed to be: Is it a satire of postmodernism? A postmodern masterpiece? Is it the diary of a North Korean mamasan? Maybe it reveals the most arcane secrets of Freemasonry. Maybe sacred geometry exists within the numerology of each chapter. Maybe it doubles as a map for the treasure I buried. Maybe none. Maybe all.

This is for me to know and you to discover.

I thank you all sincerely for reading and hope you will continue to follow me on my writing journey long into the future.

CREDITS

Author
Pablo Weston

Graphic Designer
Nhi Nguyen

Printed in Great Britain
by Amazon